Dear Parents and Educators,

Welcome to Penguin Young Readers! As parents and educators, you know that each child develops at his or her own pace—in terms of speech, critical thinking, and, of course, reading. Penguin Young Readers recognizes this fact. As a result, each Penguin Young Readers book is assigned a traditional easy-to-read level (1–4) as well as a Guided Reading Level (A–P). Both of these systems will help you choose the right book for your child. Please refer to the back of each book for specific leveling information. Penguin Young Readers features esteemed authors and illustrators, stories about favorite characters, fascinating nonfiction, and more!

Alexander Hamilton: American Hero

LEVEL **4**

GUIDED READING LEVEL **N**

This book is perfect for a **Fluent Reader** who:
• can read the text quickly with minimal effort;
• has good comprehension skills;
• can self-correct (can recognize when something doesn't sound right); and
• can read aloud smoothly and with expression.

Here are some **activities** you can do during and after reading this book:
• Nonfiction: Nonfiction books deal with facts and events that are real. Talk about the elements of nonfiction, and make a list of facts about Alexander Hamilton that you learned in this book.
• Research: Alexander Hamilton is considered a Founding Father of the United States of America. Do some research on other famous Founding Fathers. Choose one and write a paragraph about him.

Remember, sharing the love of reading with a child is the best gift you can give!

—Sarah Fabiny, Editorial Director
   Penguin Young Readers program

D0091978

*Penguin Young Readers are leveled by independent reviewers applying th[...] [...]unds and Gay Su Pinnell in *Matching Books to Readers: Using Leveled Books in Guided Reading*, Heinemann, 1999.

For Bob, Darlene, Jess, Bryan, Rob,
and Lara—BL

This book is for my little brother—GE

PENGUIN YOUNG READERS
An Imprint of Penguin Random House LLC

Penguin supports copyright. Copyright fuels creativity, encourages diverse voices,
promotes free speech, and creates a vibrant culture. Thank you for buying an authorized edition
of this book and for complying with copyright laws by not reproducing, scanning, or distributing any part
of it in any form without permission. You are supporting writers and allowing Penguin to
continue to publish books for every reader.

The publisher does not have any control over and does not assume any responsibility
for author or third-party websites or their content.

Text copyright © 2018 by Barbara Lowell. Illustrations copyright © 2018 by Penguin Random House LLC.
All rights reserved. Published by Penguin Young Readers, an imprint of Penguin Random House LLC,
345 Hudson Street, New York, New York 10014. Manufactured in China.

Library of Congress Cataloging-in-Publication Data is available.

ISBN 9781524787738 (pbk)   10 9 8 7 6 5 4 3 2 1
ISBN 9781524787745 (hc)   10 9 8 7 6 5 4 3 2 1

Alexander Hamilton
American Hero

by Barbara Lowell
illustrated by George Ermos

Penguin Young Readers
An Imprint of Penguin Random House

Alexander Hamilton is an American
hero. But he wasn't born in America.

Alexander was born on Nevis, in the Caribbean. A bright blue sea circled the island.

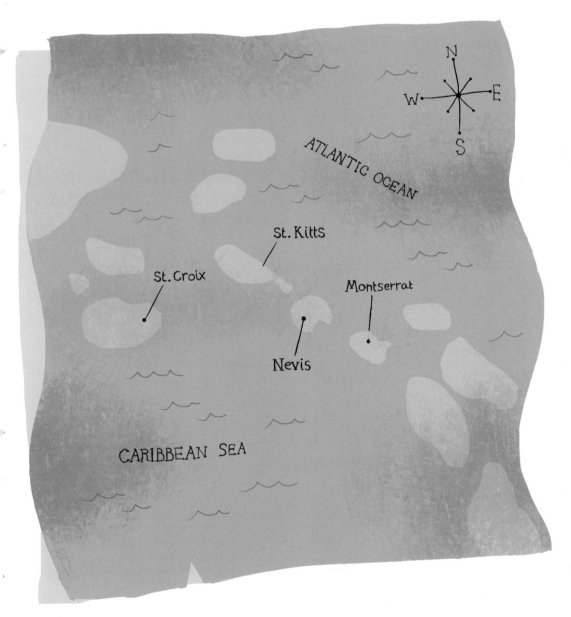

When Alexander was 10, his family moved to St. Croix. Then his father left. Alexander never saw him again.

His mother opened a store. Alexander helped her run it.

When he wasn't working, he liked
to read his mother's books. He read
about the heroes of Greece and Rome.

Alexander's mother died when he was 13. Alexander was now an orphan.

Everything his mother owned was sold.
But his uncle saved his mother's books
for him.

Alexander went to work for a shipping company.

When he was 16, his boss took a trip to America. Alexander ran the business. He told ship captains what to do.

After five months, his boss came back. Alexander was no longer in charge. He wished for a better life.

Then a big storm hit the island.
Alexander wrote about it. He said the
sea and wind roared. He said houses
crashed to the ground.

Alexander's story was in the newspaper. People said he was smart. They raised money to send him to school in America.

Alexander packed his books. He sailed to his new home.

Alexander went to a school in New York City. He met American patriots. They wanted the British king's rule to end in America.

Alexander joined them. He wrote
about freedom. He spoke against
British rule. Alexander was a hero
to the patriots.

The British king sent soldiers
to America. They met patriots ready
to fight. Both sides fired their guns.
The Revolutionary War had begun.

Alexander left school. He joined
the army as a captain.

British ships sailed up a river
in New York. Alexander and his men
fired their cannons at the ships.

Alexander was fighting for America's freedom. He was in many battles early in the war. His men looked up to him as a leader.

General George Washington saw
Alexander in action. He thought
Alexander was daring and brave.
He asked for his help.

Alexander wrote Washington's letters.
He read reports from American spies.
He rode into battle with Washington.

At the Battle of Yorktown, Alexander
led his men in a charge.

A wall guarded the British soldiers.
They fired their guns at the Americans.

Alexander jumped over the wall.
He yelled to his men to follow him and
fight.

The British waved the white flag.
They gave up. Americans won their
freedom.

Americans were free. But America was not a country like it is today. The states didn't work together.

Alexander helped write the Constitution. Under its rules, the states would work together. Only then could America become a strong country.

Not all the states liked it. So Alexander wrote about how important it was. He helped Americans understand it.

Then all thirteen states voted for the Constitution.

Americans chose George Washington as their president.

He needed a smart secretary of the treasury. This person would work on everything having to do with America's money.

Washington picked Alexander. Alexander said, with this job, "I can do the most good."

Alexander set up a national bank.
It handled America's money.

He formed a coast guard. The people
on its ships managed which goods came
into the country.

He called for a United States Mint
to make American money.

Alexander helped build a strong
America.

A man named Aaron Burr was
running for governor of New York.
Alexander said he did not trust him.

Burr was angry. He asked for a duel,
a fight using guns.

Alexander said yes. He believed
in honor.

Alexander fired his gun into the air,
not at Burr. Burr shot Alexander.

The next day, Alexander died.

Alexander Hamilton sailed to America a poor boy from the Caribbean.

He became a patriot, a soldier, and a Founding Father.

He helped form America's government. His ideas about money made the country strong.

Alexander Hamilton is one of America's greatest heroes.